Enjoy the *Journey*

A Woman's

Guide to Retirement

Elaine & Scott Manley

FINANCIAL JOURNEY
PARTNERS
Partners in Your Financial Journey.

Disclosures

The information contained in the book is intended to provide general information for educational purposes only, as investment recommendations and decisions must consider your specific facts and circumstances. This material should not be construed as an offer of, or recommendation of, any security, nor should it be construed as offering investment advice nor be viewed as an advertisement for advisory services. The views expressed are those of the authors and do not necessarily reflect the views of Mutual Advisors, LLC or Mutual Securities, Inc. and any of its affiliates.

Financial Journey Partners Logo, Partners in Your Financial Journey, and FJP Retirement Framework are registered trademarks of Financial Journey Partners, Inc. Any unauthorized use is expressly prohibited.

Certified Financial Planner Board of Standards, Inc. (CFP Board) owns the CFP® certification mark, the CERTIFIED FINANCIAL PLANNER™ certification mark, and the CFP® certification mark (with plaque design) logo in the United States, which it authorizes use of by individuals who successfully complete CFP Board's initial and ongoing certification requirements.

Contents

enjoying your hobbies you have wanted to do for years? Maybe it is all the above. We want the thought of retirement to bring you joy and pleasure from all the amazing possibilities of things you plan to do, during the remainder of your life.

This book is specifically written for women who are planning to retire in the next few years and for women who are already in retirement. We want to help guide you through the process of preparing and implementing your retirement so you can achieve your goals and dreams. We want you to live a fulfilling and enjoyable life in retirement.

As we mentioned, we wrote another book to share the details for planning and implementing a plan for retirement. The book *Enjoy the Journey, Successful Retirement Strategies and Stories* goes into more detail about the process we use to help anyone transitioning from working full-time to the next phase of their life. It is available on Amazon in eBook, paperback, and hard cover.

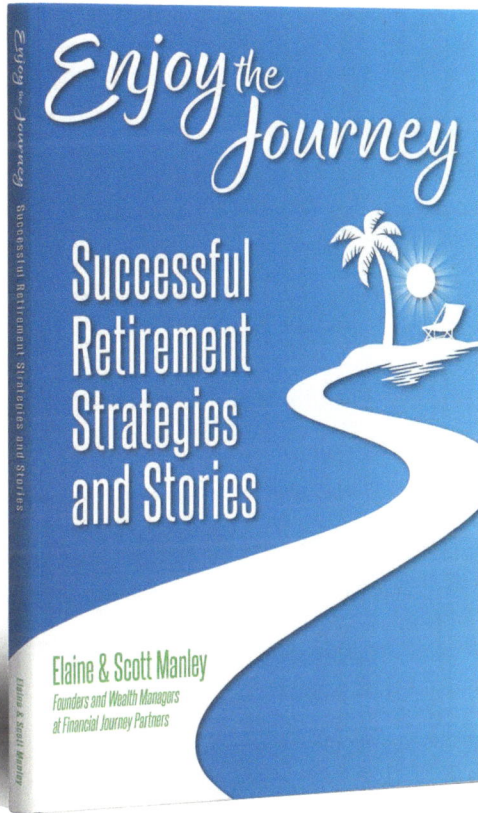

The book includes real client stories of people that have made the successful transition to retirement. It also includes exercises to help you think through the important decisions when making this transition. You can download a complimentary workbook to use when completing the exercises in the book at the website www.financialjourney.com/books.

How do I make a complex situation work smoothly?

Cheryl was a very successful HR professional and later a consultant. She amassed a significant amount of wealth, mostly in the stock of one company. Dealing with the early loss of her husband and then having to overcome cancer, she had been tested and had come out the other side. She created a life full of family and friends, along with enough money to do what she wants.

Thoughtful and caring, she is passionate about helping her family and her community. Giving back to organizations she cares deeply about was important in her financial planning. Cheryl has handled so much on her own. She recognizes the importance of having the right professionals on her team, who will objectively advise, guide and help her with the things she doesn't want to do herself. We helped her understand all her different assets and how she can use them to create the lifestyle she wants. Then we consolidated and organized her finances and built a plan to best position her financial assets for her desired retirement lifestyle. We created a retirement income distribution strategy as well as a strategy for her company stock and charitable goals.

As we go through the years together, we collaborate on how to optimize her taxes, gifting regularly to her family and charities and keep the cashflow going for her. With homes in two states, she is able to live in her paradise and visit her family when she wants. She's living the life she creates and handling things very well. Having us on her team, gives her the information she needs to make smart decisions and reduces the stress of managing all these moving parts. It is a unique retirement plan, and it fits her very well.

"Elaine and her team have been critical to the planning and execution of the financial aspects of retirement. She has supported me through not only the financial aspects of retirement planning but emotional aspects. As trusted advisors they have provided sage advice and knowledgeable options that give me the peace of mind that I'm on the right track. I sleep better knowing that Elaine is on top of my financial plan and looking after my best interests."

1: Risks to Minimize

Women's Words of Wisdom

It's only money. – C.W.

Let's take a few moments and look at some of the risks involved in retirement decisions. This chapter will cover some of the most significant risks in retirement decisions. Some of them are "blind spots" meaning the person is not aware of the risk. We bring it to your attention so you can evaluate if this is something you may need to handle as you prepare or continue your retirement.

When a woman comes to us for the first time as a prospective client, we start by asking lots of questions and listening carefully to get to know her very well. We want to know her values, goals, concerns, important relationships, assets, professional advisors, and hobbies. We want to help people reach their goals faster than they thought was possible.

What we typically find is that the person has some areas that can dramatically impede the success of their plan or even result in failure. Let's discuss some of the common ones that we have seen.

HANDS ON VERSUS HANDS OFF

When you think about your retirement, you may be thinking to yourself:
- "I have no idea what to do next so I'll just leave it alone."
- "I can save a little money if I do it myself."
- "I don't want to look like I need help."
- "I had a successful working career, so I can do this on my own."

We had a woman client tell us "My female friends just want to do it themselves. They don't want any help." She shrugged and said "I'd much rather work with you and know that I'm doing things the right way for my situation." These women may be having different levels of success. Our experience has shown that there are likely areas that could be done better if they had experienced professionals helping them. Ignoring your investments and not developing an overall plan, can set you or your heirs on a path with more challenges than opportunities. Do you really want to risk the success of your retirement plan on someone who is doing this for the first time – you?

TOO MUCH RISK

A common mistake is having too much risk in the investments in their portfolio. Some investors leave their money invested in stocks, whether the stock market is going up or down, because they say, "the stock market always recovers". The U.S. stock market fell 50% from 2000 to 2002 and again from 2008 to 2009. It took years for the stock market to recover from these losses. If a person is retired and taking money out of their accounts to live on, while the stock market is down significantly, there may not be time to let their investments recover. We have found accounts, bank accounts, or real estate may have never been retitled properly to be included in the trust.

No estate plan: Some people can come up with reason after reason to delay getting an estate plan. We have seen situations with people passing away with no estate plan and the family is left with a unnecessarily bad situation, that will take years to be resolved in the Probate Court. Those with real estate ended up spending more than $100,000 to settle their estate. Another person with real estate and private company stock spent 3 years and hundreds of thousands of dollars in attorney and estate fees. We highly recommend you have an estate plan and make sure it is updated on a regular basis. You may have heard the expression – "Don't be penny wise and pound foolish." It is well worth paying a good estate planning attorney to make sure your documents are in good order to help make things easier on your heirs.

Wrong trustee: A common practice in estate plans is to list a family member as the trustee for their estate. While it may seem like a good idea at the time, we have seen situations where this is very problematic. The family member chosen to be the trustee may not have the time, interest, or skills to complete all the activities required by the trustee to settle the estate. It may be much better to hire a professional fiduciary to handle these duties.

MONEY "SCATTERED"

Another common unintended mistake that we find is people have changed jobs over their career and they have 401k accounts left behind from their many past jobs. The person is usually not managing the money in these accounts and the money can end up with investments that do very poorly. Even worse, what happens to this retirement account if the company goes out of business? We recommend that people move the money in 401(k)s at previous employers to their 401(k) account at their current employer. Another good option may be to roll over the 401(k) account at past employers to one IRA rollover account. Keeping your retirement assets consolidated simplifies your financial life. It is usually much easier to manage all the money in one account than trying to handle 7 or 8 different accounts.

OVERSPENDING

We have observed some people retire and quickly find activities that make them happy and give them purpose to their life. We have seen other people retire, without clear goals or activities to fill their day, and they become bored, and they are unhappy. We have seen retired people with too much time on their hands, so they find themselves shopping and travelling more than they can afford.

TOO MUCH TIME TOGETHER

Some couples that retire tell us they are driving each other crazy. A client recently told us "Will it drive me crazy to have my retired husband home all day?" This can put strain on the relationship. We believe it is important for a couple to have a heart-to-heart conversation about how to best spend their time together, as changes occur with their situation.

TOO LITTLE TIME TOGETHER

For a couple, what happens if one person retires and the other keeps working? The person that retires can become bored as they wait months

Exercise:
Risks to Minimize

Instructions: We discussed some of the risks that can prevent you from achieving your goals and living the retirement of your dreams. List the risks you are aware of in your situation. If your first reaction is "I don't have any risks in my situation", then we suggest you think about this more and perhaps even talk about this with your family members or friends. You may have blind spots to issues that you are not aware of. Here are some common risks as examples to consider, then list the areas you may have risks in your situation.

Examples:
- No estate plan or incomplete estate plan.
- Too much or too little risk in investments.
- No goals in retirement.
- Amount of time together for a couple.

Risks to Minimize?

_____

_____

_____

_____

_____

_____

of mind to know that they will have enough money and will not run out of money in their lifetime.

Once the women reach the point of financial independence, their focus often shifts to health. Their top goal is now being healthy so they can live a long life and be able to accomplish all their goals during retirement. We have seen this over the decades of working with women and we see this confirmed in our recent survey.

In the survey, we wanted to learn more about the concerns women have when they end their full-time working career, so we asked the question a little differently. We asked the question "What do you think is the number one thing that you are most concerned about that could keep you from living the retirement of your dreams?" It was an open-ended question so they could answer it in their own words.

Q2: *What do you think is the number one thing that you are most concerned about that could keep you from living the retirement of your dreams?*

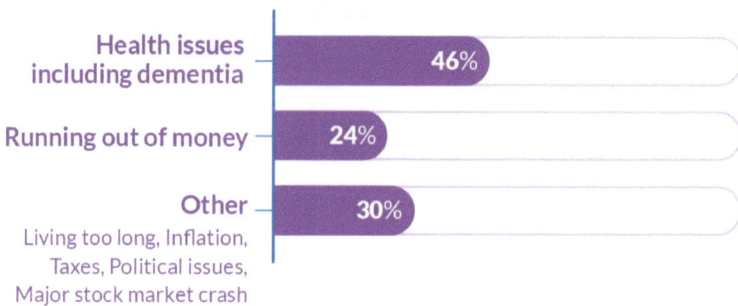

Health issues including dementia — **46%**

Running out of money — **24%**

Other — **30%**
Living too long, Inflation, Taxes, Political issues, Major stock market crash

The answers were consistent with the previous question that had a limited set of answers. Forty six percent of the women answered with something related to their health. They were concerned that health issues would keep them from living the retirement of their dreams. They were worried about having a medical emergency that would cost them a lot of money. They were also concerned about declining mental abilities, such as dementia.

As in the prior question, the second most common answer after concerns about health was concern about running out of money. Interestingly enough, we've heard several women say they were worried about becoming a "bag lady". This can be a deep-rooted fear for some women. With our financial planning tools, we can show women they are going to be OK. And yes, there is a risk of running out of money for anyone that spends beyond their means.

The remaining answers were spread across a range of different types of concerns.

- Losing my spouse/partner
- Geopolitical concerns and elections
- Economic concerns such as inflation
- Finding interesting things to do
- Being able to travel as much as I would like
- High state taxes
- Having a child or partner with special needs

The next step is to start addressing the top concerns expressed by the women in the survey. In the next chapter, we will begin by discussing ideas for staying healthy in retirement.

Rochelle said *"Before meeting Elaine and Scott, I had finally rid myself of that fear after having saved a fair amount of money. However, it wasn't until they became our financial advisors that I finally felt secure with the thought of retirement with more than adequate resources to address spending needs and charitable giving. With the comprehensive retirement plan and regular investment meetings, it gave me the peace of mind to knowing that I would be fine."*

She is passionate about contributing to her favorite charities. The question in her financial plan was how much the appropriate amount was to donate to her favorite charities, yet still be able to reach her other retirement goals. Elaine met with Rochelle and the representatives for the charities. We did some scenarios using the financial plan and together we determined the appropriate amount to donate to the charities. This was accomplished while keeping Rochelle and her husband on track with her remaining goals.

Today they spend their time with their two dogs, friends, family, and contributing to their favorite charities. Rochelle and her husband still help a few clients with their commercial real estate needs while having time to *Enjoy the Journey.*

Exercise:
My Biggest Concerns

Instructions: Whether you are planning for retirement, or already retired, what are your top concerns that could keep you from living the retirement of your dreams? What are the concerns that could keep you up at night worrying about them? Make a list of these concerns below. Then give each concern a number for their priority, starting with 1 as your top concern.

Concern	Rank Concerns

An area of growing concern as we age is dementia and the more severe Alzheimer's. In the past, there were many things that caused people to die at younger ages. With modern medicine, people are living longer, and more people are experiencing different types of mental decline. Having a long and healthy retirement is not just staying health physically, it is also staying sharp mentally.

We have discussed ways to try and stay healthy during retirement. It is important to have a good medical insurance plan in the event you have an illness. If you were employed with a major corporation, then you likely had a medical insurance plan through your employer. This is significantly cheaper than getting a plan on your own since your employer was likely paying for some of your medical plan.

When you turn 65, you are eligible for Medicare. Whether you are still working or not at age 65, you are required to register for Medicare. You can register up to 3 months before 65, or until 3 months after. If you are still working, you will likely continue to use your company medical plan. It's very important that you work with your HR department a couple of months before turning 65 to understand their procedures for your medical coverage. If you are retired at 65, then you will use Medicare. When on Medicare, you should consider buying a Medicare Supplement Insurance to pay for the healthcare that is not covered by Medicare. There are also Medicare Advantage plans but there are also risks if you ever have an expensive illness. You may not have the coverage you expected with the Advantage plans so be sure to research the pros and cons before making your decision.

The Medicare Supplement plans often change each year, and the details vary from company to company. We recommend you work with a Medicare Specialist to help you find the supplemental insurance plan that is best for you. Since plans may differ by state, we recommend you work with a Medicare Specialist in your local area. These professionals are normally paid a commission by the insurance companies and their services are normally free to the consumer. Make a Medicare Specialist a part of your team of professionals.

LONGEVITY

One of the key questions in developing a financial plan is "How long do you think you will live?" We believe the best way to determine whether a person could run out of money during retirement is to do a comprehensive financial plan that is unique to the person's situation. A comprehensive financial plan includes the person's goals, expenses, income and financial assets. A financial plan spans the time from today, to the remainder of the person's life, or until the age that is assumed they will pass. To complete such a financial plan, it is necessary to select a life expectancy age for the person, or the age at which they will pass.

Greater numbers of people are living into their 90's and even reaching age 100 and beyond. Many different factors can enable a person to live longer or cause them to pass prematurely. Selecting a life expectancy age for the end of a financial plan is an important part of the planning process. Completing the financial plan for the person to live until age 80 will yield very different results than a financial plan for a woman assumed to live until age 100.

Selecting a life expectancy age that is significantly different from what occurs can result in problems. For example, assume a person creates a financial plan for them to live until age 100, yet they end up passing

Exercise:
Longevity Planning

Instructions: When creating your financial plan, it is necessary to select a date for the end of your plan. This is your age at the end of your life. Your financial plan is created to make sure you have enough money to last to the end of your life. Everyone is different and unexpected things can happen, but it is helpful to select the best age possible for how long you expect to live. Livingto100.com is a free website that asks 40 questions to give you an estimate for how long you may live. It takes about 10 minutes to complete these questions.

1 What is your life expectancy age from the Livingto100.com Life Expectancy calculator?

_____

2 List reasons specific to your situation why you think you might live shorter than the answer from the calculator.

_____

3 List reasons specific to your situation why you think you might live longer than the answer from the calculator.

_____

4 Select your life expectancy age from the questions above that you want to be used in your financial plan.

_____

is one of the most common errors that can cause someone to run out of money in retirement.

Yes, you can track your spending and expenses manually. That would be time consuming and tedious. Happily, there is a better option. There is software available to daily download your spending transactions from your credit card and checking account. Then you can categorize your expenses and compare your spending each month to your target set for each category. It's part of our financial planning software program. It's also available through other firms like Intuit Quicken. There are other firms offering "free" software, but realize they may be selling your information. So please track your spending and we recommend you select software that will keep your personal data safe, while making it easy for you.

People can live for 30 or more years in retirement. Imagine living almost as many years in retirement as you had in your working career. When your retirement lasts for so many years, spending more than your financial plan target is magnified over all those years. In other words, overspending, especially in the early years of your retirement, can have an increasingly large negative impact over all the years of your retirement.

THE MARKETS

We talked about this earlier, but it's important to say it again. Another potential problem that can cause you to run out of money during retirement is to have too much risk with your investments. The US stock market had large corrections downward during the Dotcom Bubble in 2000 – 2002, The Great Financial Crisis in 2008 – 2009 and Covid Pandemic in 2020 – 2021. Some sectors of the US stock market fell 50% or more during these periods.

When a person is working and adding to their retirement savings, they have time for their accounts to recover and grow before they retire. If a person is retired and withdrawing money out of their accounts to pay living expenses, there may not be time for the investments to recover. Withdrawing money for living expenses while the market is trending down during a large market correction can have a very damaging effect on your retirement assets.

The person's financial plan may have said they had enough money to last through their retirement. They may find that after a large market correction they are at risk of running out of money. When markets are in a significant correction, it is helpful to reduce spending as much as possible. Another solution is to ensure that your assets are invested in a way to be able to ride through market corrections, so you do not run out of money. If you are not sure how to do this, then we recommend you talk with a financial professional.

Something to remember about 401(k) accounts is they were designed to be a convenient way for employees to save monthly for their retirement. These accounts allow money to be taken out of their paycheck each month and automatically deposited into their retirement account by their employer. Once you retire, you are normally not able to withdraw money each month from a 401(k) to pay for living expenses. When people retire and want to start making monthly withdrawals, people normally rollover their money to a rollover Individual Retirement Account (IRA).

There are several solutions to handle this problem of money left behind in 401(k) accounts at previous employers. Most 401(k) plans allow money from other companies from previous jobs to be rolled into the new company 401(k) plan. We believe this is better than leaving money in

When balancing the needs of work and family, when is the best time to retire?

Lee worked as the HR Director for several companies. During this time, she raised two kids as a single Mom after a difficult divorce. After the kids were grown and progressing in their respective careers, she was the caregiver for her aging Mother for several years. Lee balanced the needs of her family as well as work and was able to be successful in both areas.

When Lee first met Elaine about 20 years ago, she was hoping she could retire. When we created her financial plan for retirement, her plan showed it would lead to a very frugal retirement. But if she worked a few more years, the picture was much brighter. She found a great job at a great firm, and she was able to accumulate more assets in just a few years. At that point, we were both confident in her financial income sources and she chose to retire.

We developed a budget, and she was excellent at tracking her expenses and making adjustments as needed. In reviewing what she enjoyed doing over the years, she spotted an opportunity to work for a nonprofit that she really admired, and she now gets paid to help them! This has been such a wonderful experience for her. She is more fulfilled and of course this work enhanced her retirement income.

And it gets better – now she's found love again later in life and is having a great time with her new "boyfriend". She works part time with her nonprofit, visits with her family in LA and enjoys her time with her beau. She is living her dream life.

5: I Didn't Know That!

Words of Wisdom

There is always more to learn. – Elaine Manley

The survey of our women clients told us that the top two concerns for our women clients related to their retirement are staying healthy in retirement and not running out of money. We discussed those in detail in the last two chapters. Other concerns listed by the women in the survey included:

- Inflation
- Political and geopolitical events
- Losing my spouse/partner
- When should I sell my house
- Finding things that I have interest in
- Being able to travel as much as I want
- Investment returns
- High state taxes

Our women clients shared their many concerns with us. Having a comprehensive financial plan in place can help reduce many of these concerns.

What if there are risks that you don't even know about? We have found that people planning for retirement without the help of an experience professional, may have risks and issues they simply do not know about. It could just be "I don't know what I don't know". By working with an experienced professional, they can help make sure you know what you need to know for your situation.

In this chapter, we will start by discussing some of the most common issues that our Wealth Managers find with new clients. The following are a list of topics that people should consider.

FORGOT TO UPDATE THE DEED

Recently, a couple became new clients. The man had gotten divorced and some years later he remarried. His house had been purchased with his first wife and the title for the house was in the name of the man and his first wife. When the man remarried, he didn't think to change the title on his house. Had he passed away, the house would have gone to his first wife. His current wife would have been kicked out of the house. This was not what the man had in mind. After discovering that the title for the house had not been updated after the divorce, he quickly worked with an estate attorney. He updated the title to remove his first wife and add his current wife. Close call!

them "What are some situations related to retirement that I didn't know I didn't know until I actually retired and experienced this situation?"

LOSS OF A SPOUSE/PARTNER

Our client's husband passed a few years ago. Some of the financial things had been taken care of in the past by her husband and she had to learn how to do them. In addition, there were many more things she had to deal with. Her husband's IRA had to be retitled into her name. She had to contact the life insurance company to claim the death benefit for her husband's life insurance policy.

Social Security needed to be notified of her husband's death to evaluate the claim to determine what her Social Security benefit would be going forward. She was surprised how much was involved financially when she was dealing with the death of her husband. The passing of a spouse is an emotionally difficult period. We have helped our clients many times through the financial decisions and actions that must be taken at this stressful time.

INSURANCES

A woman client was planning for her retirement. She had life insurance but did not have long-term care insurance. She was wondering if when she retires, she should have life insurance, long term care insurance, or both. There is no easy answer here. Because everyone's situation is different, the answer is not the same for everyone. This is where it is important to talk with a professional about the options and your situation.

We believe it is important to complete a comprehensive financial plan to determine how life insurance and long-term care insurance fit into this plan. Important factors to consider include how much can you afford to pay for both life insurance and long-term care insurance after you retire. It would not be wise to pay so much for these insurances that the person runs the risk of running out of money later in life.

HOW TO SHIFT FROM SAVINGS TO SPENDING

During the working portion of your life, a primary objective is to save and accumulate money to have enough to last through all the years of your retirement. A woman client told us that it was hard for her to shift from saving money when working, to a focus of not spending too much money after retiring. We help our clients develop a budget for spending during their retirement years. This gives them a clear idea of what they can spend and still not run out of money in their lifetime.

We also encourage people to use an online budgeting tool to download and track your expenses to help you monitor and make sure your spending is in line with your budget. We provide advanced online budgeting software for our clients. This software makes the process of tracking your budget much easier. We worked with our client to create a financial plan that includes her assets, spending, and goals. Her plan shows that she will have enough money to last the rest of her life. She told us that seeing her projected financial plan with enough money for the rest of her life greatly reduced the stress caused by this major shift.

NEVER TOO EARLY TO START PLANNING

A young woman client of ours that still has many years until her retirement, was surprised to learn that she should start planning for retirement, even though it is many years away. We recommend people start a 401(k) as soon as they start their first job after college. The longer a person waits to start saving and planning for retirement, the more difficult it becomes to save enough for retirement. We believe it is never too early to start planning for retirement.

ENJOYING RETIREMENT

On the positive side, some of our women clients also tell us that they didn't know how great retirement would be. One woman told us if she had known how great retirement would be for her, that she would have retired earlier. Another woman told us "I didn't know that this stage of life would be so enriching, freeing, wonderful, open to discovering my REAL self, and unconstrained by imposed expectations of what I had to be and do."

Expanding What is Possible

How do we know if we can afford all our goals and travel that we want to do during our retirement?

Lily walked into a high school party and heard this guy playing the guitar. She took one look at him, and it was love at first sight. They dated for a couple of years and married at a young age. Amazingly, they bought their first house when they were just 19. She worked as a hairdresser for a few years and then was able to stay home and raise their children. Zach worked as a surveyor with a Civil Engineering company. He worked there for 27 years and eventually became a partner in 1990. They worked hard and saved their money. They bought rental properties over the years and did very well. He also fully funded his retirement with their Profit Sharing plan at work. That enabled them to retire earlier than most.

Lily and her husband Zack had been used to saving their money. They were very careful with their spending. Their first financial advisor never ran a plan for them. He just sold them an investment and they never heard from him again. They thought they were ok, but they weren't certain at this stage.

Fortunately, Zack's parents had been working with us. When his mom's health started to fail, she told them it was important to talk with us. When they saw what we did for his parents, they felt they needed to

6: Living a Purposeful Life in Retirement

Words of Wisdom

Continue to make a contribution to my community. – J.O.

Seek new things. – C.L.

According to Dictionary.com, the definition of retirement is "the act of retiring or of leaving one's job, career or occupation permanently, usually because of age." The interesting thing is that the definition does not say anything about what a person does in retirement after leaving their job.

From our experience, we have noticed that people have very different thoughts about the word retirement. Some of our clients have told us that retirement to them means to stop working. Some people may view this as a time in their life when they are unproductive, without goals and bored. Other clients view retirement as a transition from a career working forty or more hours a week doing things dictated by their employer, to being able to fill their days with the things they enjoy most.

Are you dreading retirement, or are you looking forward to it? You may be a person that loved your job and the respect that people gave you in your job because of your responsibilities and acquired knowledge. Letting go of the position, title and respect can be a difficult transition for some people.

On the other hand, you may be a person who is unhappy in your job, and you are counting down the days to retirement. Your job may be causing you unwanted stress. You may have a difficult manager that is taking the fun out of your job. You may be a person that is tired of the long hours taking orders from someone else and you're ready to take on your own challenges.

It is an amazing opportunity for you to make your retirement whatever you want. You are moving from the working phase of your life, where you do the things you have to do, to the retirement phase of your life where you can do the things you want to do. You are in control of your time and activities in the retirement phase of your life.

People have very different views of what life looks in retirement after leaving their career and full-time job. The idea of retirement may range from spending too much time watching TV to having enough time to start a second career. The range of activities people want to do in their retirement can vary considerably.

Whatever you decide to do in retirement, we recommend that it include activities that give purpose to your life in retirement. Activities both physically and mentally. We believe happiness is the journey, as well as the destination. We think this starts by a person having a clear purpose and set of goals when they retire. We will talk about this more in Chapter 6. People that retire with a purpose and with defined goals tend to keep themselves busier in retirement. They are happier in retirement, and they also tend to live longer.

We asked our women clients in the survey "When you think about how you want to spend your time in retirement, rank these areas in order of importance." They are listed below with the most important at the top and least important at the bottom.

Q4: **When you think about how you want to spend your time in retirement, rank these areas in order of importance.**

Most Important

1 — Spending time with family and friends

2 — Exercising and getting in shape to stay health

3 — Personal time to do my favorite hobbies

4 — Traveling

5 — Volunteering

6 — Other

Least Important

Not surprisingly, spending time with family and friends was the most important choice for this question. This makes it important to determine the most important people in your life and to decide how much time to spend with each. Once you identify the most important people in your life, consider having a conversation with them, that goes something like this.

"I was thinking about who are the most important people in my life and you are definitely one of the most important people in my life. I want to make sure that I am spending the right amount of time with you. How much time would you like me to spend with you each week (or month)?" How do we create a plan that makes us both happy? We had this conversation with our family members. First, they felt honored to know that they are one of the most important people in our life. Next, once you find out how much time they want you to spend with them, you may already be spending enough time with them. This provides peace of mind and avoids any guilty feelings about not spending enough time with them. This creates a more fulfilling relationship for all involved.

After deciding who are the most important people in your life, then it is important to consider where you live, and if that is the best place for you to live when you retire. If the most important people in your life live in other cities, maybe it is time to consider moving closer to those people. In the later years of your life, you may need the help of your children and other family members for your care. It may make sense to move close to those people before you grow older and the physical and emotional impact of moving make it more difficult.

You have many options that include working out in a gym, hiking, playing pickleball or walking your dog. We encourage you to find activities you enjoy doing every week.

How do I donate to my favorite charities in an easy and tax efficient way?

Ellen graduated from Stanford and climbed the ladder of success in the field of education. To this day, she still does consulting and shares her knowledge regularly. Over the years of her retirement she has traveled, spent time with family and friends, and has discovered her "real" self, instead of the expectations of what she had to be and do. She is loving life, and she is making a difference.

One of the things we've helped her accomplish is optimizing her donations to her favorite charities. She uses a portion of the Required Minimum Distribution (RMD) from her retirement account to support a dozen causes she cares about the most. It's given her the sense of fulfillment and of course it has helped those charities significantly. These are called Qualified Charitable Distributions or QCDs. Her tax person had not mentioned it to her, but we did. And she has increased them each year as it helps her lower her taxes and helps her favorite organizations.

She told us *"Elaine has taught me so much. I never knew what RMD meant, and Elaine helped me realize that I have to withdraw a significant amount of RMD. My father worked for the Internal Revenue*

Service, so I never felt badly about paying taxes because that's what our family grew up on. But Elaine helped me see that there was an alternative that I could allocate some of my RMD for charitable contributions. Elaine's favorite phrase is "do some good in the world" and I am glad I can do that."

Creating My Future

	This Month	*This Year*	*In 3 Years*	*Before I'm Done*
Experience				
Growth				
Contribution				
Fun				
More				

You may need to ask this last question several times to get to your higher purpose or meaning.

An important part of getting clear on your values is deciding "What relationships matter the most to me?" We encourage you to look at the important people in your life and determine how you want to include them in your life. Once retired, you may have more time to spend with them, with opportunities not available while you were working.

After gaining clarity on your values and what is important to you, now it's time to think about your goals as far out as you can envision. We're talking about goals in all areas of your life. This includes goals for yourself, your family, your friends, the groups you belong to, your finances, the causes you are passionate about, and all other areas of your life. When creating your goals, we encourage you to think big and plan big!

Now that you have created your goals for retirement, it is time for a plan. This will help you determine your cash flow needed to pay your living expenses and fund all your goals. We want to make sure you have enough money to last the rest of your life, so you do not run out of money. We believe the best way to do this is to develop a comprehensive financial plan. The software we use allows you to include the many details in your specific situation, plus evaluate scenarios to help you make important decisions.

After saving money for your retirement, it is important to develop a plan to position those assets so that they can provide you monthly income to pay your bills during retirement. There are many strategies for doing this. This includes drawing money from Social Security, taking money out of retirement accounts and non-retirement accounts. It is important to consider the tax consequences of different strategies. Again, we believe the best way to optimize your available assets is by creating a comprehensive financial plan that is tailored to your specific situation.

The stock and bond market can fluctuate significantly with a global financial crisis, a pandemic, recessions, and large swings in interest rates. It is important to have a process to manage your investments through the up and down markets. If your investments fall significantly while you are taking money out monthly to pay for your living expenses, it may be difficult for them to recover. We believe in the active management of investments to adjust investments based on the conditions in the markets. Whether you manage your investments yourself, or have them managed by a financial professional, we would encourage you to have a strategy for managing your investments through all types of markets.

When retiring, some people have life insurance that they purchased earlier in life and the life insurance was designed to last their entire life. Some people paid for life insurance through their employer at work and it ends when they leave the company. The question people may have is "Should I keep my life insurance when I retire?" The answer is "It depends". There is not one answer for everyone. Answering this question properly should include a discussion with an experienced life insurance agent to determine if keeping your life insurance is appropriate for your situation. We have seen some situations where keeping your life insurance makes sense and other situations where it does not. We recommend working with an experienced insurance professional to help make the best decision for a person's specific situation.

Do I have all the pieces in place in my retirement plan for me to achieve my goals?

Christina worked at a tech company for several decades, becoming a highly valued technical expert at that company. When we met, she knew she had accomplished a lot but wasn't sure her funds would last until age 100. We had a detailed and meaningful discussion about her values regarding money, as well as her financial goals.

She had a lot she wanted to do and wanted to make sure she wouldn't run out of money before age 100. We transitioned her investments to align with her values and goals. We also reviewed her cash flow and developed an income strategy, in collaboration with her tax professional. This included doing some Roth Conversions in her early retirement years.

She did not have life insurance nor any long-term care insurance. While there wasn't a need for the life insurance, she is at risk if she has a long-term care illness. We reviewed different ways to mitigate that risk. As she did not have heirs that really needed to inherit funds from her, she knows she can use every asset including her home as a resource should she need it.

Christina had not established an estate plan, which was something we encouraged her to complete as soon as possible. We offered to introduce her to some great estate planning attorneys. Fortunately, she had a good experience with an attorney that helped other family members and she chose to go with him. She is finalizing her estate plan in the next couple of months.

Christina is a caring person and found she could help her community significantly through the Kiwanis Club. She works on a variety of projects and currently organizes over 20 of their members to deliver the ballots safely and securely to the Registrar of Voters Office during the election season.

That's not all, she goes hiking and traveling with friends. She loves the San Francisco 49ers and the Golden State Warriors, and watches as many games as possible. She has accomplished a significant amount and has a lot more she plans to do in the years ahead. Going through our FJP Retirement Framework™, and managing her money for her, has given her the peace of mind that she's on the right track and "has her ducks in a row". Her future is full of activities, and she has the freedom to focus on those activities, rather than studying stock charts to figure out her next investment trade. Together, we've made a lot of progress in a short amount of time. It's great to see her happy and focused on what's important to her.

8: Creating a Plan for Success

> ***I didn't know how great retirement***
> ***would be. – G.F.***

In the Introduction, you determined what is important for you and your retirement plan. Everyone is unique and it is important that your retirement plan is tailored specifically to you and your situation. In Chapter 1, you considered the risks that could derail your retirement plan and keep you from reaching your goals in retirement. In Chapter 2, you documented your biggest concerns for your retirement plan. Chapter 5 was your opportunity to think about issues and concerns that you may not have thought about in the past.

We discussed how to retire and have a life full of purpose doing the things that make you and the people you love happy. When you set your goals for retirement, we want you to think big and dream big! We believe it is important to make it a better world and we hope you set goals to make this happen. We also feel strongly that it is important to *Enjoy the Journey*.

Now it is time for you to create a comprehensive retirement plan. This plan should be designed to give you the best chance to achieve your goals and address the concerns and problems that could keep you from reaching your goals. We said this earlier in the book, but we are saying it again to add emphasis. **We believe planning gives you the greatest chance for success so you can reach your goals and *Enjoy the Journey* along the way**.

A comprehensive plan includes your investment strategy, estate planning, tax mitigation, protecting your wealth through insurance, and optimizing your charitable contributions. When we surveyed our women clients, we asked them the following questions:

- How important is it to you to receive help managing your investments?
- How important is it to you to receive Estate Planning services from an Estate Planning lawyer?
- How important is it to you to receive Tax Planning services from a tax preparation professional?
- How important is it to you to receive Wealth Protection Services (for all types of insurances) from any type of insurance agent?
- How important is it to you to receive Charitable Planning services from your Wealth Manager or any other professional?

plan completed by an estate attorney in your county. Your estate plan should be updated periodically, or as significant life events occur.

The importance of receiving Tax Planning services also received a score of 83. We have found the importance of tax planning varies based on each person's situation. Some of our clients have a relatively simple situation and they do their taxes themselves. They typically use TurboTax and they are pleased with the low cost and the results. When a person's situation becomes more complex, then we see significant value from working with a tax professional. The more complex situations may include the sale of real estate, moving from one state to another, or compensation packages that include employee stock and options. This is where tax mitigation can really bring value.

Wealth protection services received a score of 67. This area includes assistance with all areas of your insurance including home, health, auto, life and long-term care. There are many things to consider across all these types of insurances to make sure you have the correct type of insurance and the correct amount of coverage. It is important to select plans and policies with the benefits best suited for your situation. Again, we recommend you find an experienced insurance professional that can help you in each of these areas. We are licensed life insurance agents and have been helping clients with life and long-term care insurance for decades. We refer people to health insurance agents and home, car, and liability insurance agents when appropriate.

The final area of the survey was services provided to help with charitable giving. This received the lowest score of 46. This is consistent with our experience that people have different interests in charitable giving and they provide charitable gifts in different amounts. This area may not keep some people from achieving their goals, but we have seen some cases where it could. For example, if someone agrees to giving a charitable gift that is too large for their amount of assets, it could financially limit the funds available for other goals. Also, if done correctly, it is important to get all the tax benefits that are legally available in the tax codes.

There are many excellent tools available to help you create a comprehensive plan for your retirement that is uniquely tailored to your situation. We would caution you against using some of the very simplistic and free software that is available. You get what you pay for and in this case, it may not be very much or even worse, the results may be wrong and not reflect your complete situation.

It is important to have a plan that accurately includes all the parts of your retirement plan, accurately reflects the taxes in your plan, and allows you to evaluate scenarios when you run into important life choices. If this is more than you can or want to do on your own, then we encourage you to find an experienced financial professional you trust with whom you can build a solid relationship. We recommend your plan includes your goals and takes into consideration risks and the concerns you listed above. And finally, once the plan is complete and it has you excited about your future, it is important to monitor your plan regularly and adjust along the way as things change in your situation.

Now let's spend time reviewing income generating ideas. Afterall, your retirement experience is based on the amount of income you can receive from all your resources.

plan that includes an analysis to determine the best time for you to begin claiming Social Security.

INCOME FROM RETIREMENT ACCOUNTS

You may have retirement savings in a 401(k) account at your employer. These are great vehicles for saving money for retirement while you are working. You can save money into a 401(k) pretax, let the money grow inside the account, and then pay taxes on the money as ordinary income when it is withdrawn. 401(k) accounts are not designed to provide automated monthly income once you retire. Most people roll over their 401(k) to an IRA and then use the IRA to send money to your bank account each month to pay your expenses. If you are saving money to your post-tax account or Roth 401(k) account inside your company's 401(k), then this money can be rolled over to your own Roth IRA.

Companies provide pensions with monthly payments for the rest of an employee's life after they retire. Today, very few public companies provide pensions for their employees. Most companies replaced pensions with 401(k)s. Federal, state, county, and city government agencies still provide pensions for many of their workers. Pensions are still common for teachers and police officers.

ANNUITIES CAN PROVIDE GUARANTEED INCOME

There are many types of annuities, and there are too many to describe here. The important point about an annuity is that it can take an amount of your money and create a monthly income that an insurance company will guarantee to pay you for the rest of your life, no matter how long you live. If you are married, an annuity can pay you a guaranteed income for as long as you or your spouse live. With pensions becoming less common, annuities can be a replacement to create a guaranteed monthly income for the rest of your life.

OTHER SOURCES OF MONTHLY INCOME

Some people are fortunate to get a sizable inheritance from parents or other family members. This money can be invested at a financial institution or bank and set up to send a monthly amount to your checking account to pay your expenses. You may have an investment account that is not an IRA that could be titled as a Trust account, a joint account with your spouse, or an individual account that is just in your name. This type of account can also be set up to send you a monthly amount to your checking account.

There are other methods of setting up monthly income, such as purchasing a rental property and using the rent you receive to pay your monthly expenses. When in the right location, that rental property could also increase in value. There are many advantages to investing in real estate. There also tends to be more complications with rentals so be sure to hire trustworthy professionals to help you with these types of investments.

With all these different ways to receive income during retirement, you may have questions such as:
- Which sources of income are best for my situation?
- If I have different sources of income, how much do I take from each?
- Which income sources should I start withdrawing from first?

Understanding your current assets, situation and goals for passing money to your beneficiaries can significantly change the strategies you use with your assets to create income for you during retirement. Your financial plan will help you see how the different scenarios can unfold to help you determine the best plan for you.

WHAT IF TAX RATES GO UP IN THE FUTURE?

Another issue that could affect your plan for income during retirement is changes in tax rates over the next several decades. The U.S. Federal Government has been running very large deficits in recent years. We think the size of these large deficits is unsustainable. If that is true, then there is a good chance that tax rates could go up in the future.

If your goal is to reduce the total amount of taxes you pay over your lifetime, then it may make sense to use more of the taxable money now (such as money in an IRA) and pay the tax on the money as it comes out of the account now, at potentially lower tax rates. Then, you can leave non-taxed money in Roth accounts and possibly lower-taxed money in non-retirement accounts for use when you are older.

WHAT ABOUR IRMAA?

IRMAA is the acronym for the income-related monthly adjustment amount. It is an extra premium that some Medicare part B and D enrollees must pay in addition to their standard Medicare premium. The Social Security Administration (SSA) determines who pays IRMAA based on their income from two years prior. The income level where you start paying IRMAA changes each year. See your tax professional for the annual thresholds.

When money comes out of your traditional IRA, it is taxed at the ordinary income rate. If you want to keep the IRMAA low, then you will need to keep the amount of money that you take out of your IRA low. Your adjusted gross income determines if, and how much, you pay for IRMAA. The IRMAA threshold is one consideration. There are other taxes you pay along the way so it may not be wise to focus on just this level of income when designing your overall tax strategy.

SHOULD I DO A ROTH CONVERSION?

A Roth Conversion takes money from your pre-tax IRA and moves it to your Roth IRA. Anyone can do a Roth conversion, regardless of income or tax filing status. A rule for Roth Conversions is that if you withdraw the converted funds less than five years after they were converted, you will have a 10% penalty on the withdrawn earnings. When you do a Roth Conversion, the amount moved from the IRA to the Roth is considered taxable income. It is added to your total taxable income for that year. It can push you above the limit and cause you to pay the additional IRMAA if you are 65 and older and paying for Medicare. Optimizing your total taxes may mean you pay more with IRMAA so you can pay less in federal taxes over the long run.

We have seen this strategy work well for people in their early retirement years. Required minimum distributions (RMDs) must come out of your IRA once you reach a certain age. Congress has been changing these ages so it's important to check with your financial or tax advisor once you reach your 70's. You may be retired, not required to take distributions

"I Feel at Peace with My Dying Process"

If I am single and do not have kids, who will help care for me when I am older?

Women who are single and do not have kids have the special challenge of finding the right person to help care for them when they are in their final years. In several families, we have seen a niece or nephew step up to fill the role. It could also be a longtime friend. Regardless of who you select, we feel it is important to have a plan for your unique situation that gives you the peace of mind that you will be well cared for as you age.

Katie has been our client for a couple of decades. At this stage in her life she said:

"I'm single and I have no children. As my death is approaching, I have large concerns about being put into a nursing facility and hating it. Elaine has helped me to put together a plan and she also included my niece, who is my executrix, so we have all of my fears and all of my desires understood and we've developed a plan to handle them. I feel at peace because my dying process is planned."

Without having the right documents in place and the right people to perform their duties, one runs the risk of being put into an undesirable situation. By coordinating with your advisor, estate planning professional, and the people that will be your successor trustee and Power of Attorney, everyone understands what is needed and has the required documentation to make it happen.

two have won the game!" … and in his next breath, he said … "now, let me show you how not to un-win it!". The retirement plan that we created together, gives Liz and Frank the freedom and confidence to enjoy the lifestyle they hoped and planned for, to enjoy their growing and extended family, as well as the ability to travel and seek out new adventures in the next chapter of their lives.

How Important Are These Services

Instructions: In this chapter, we discuss the survey of our women clients and how they rated the importance of these different services. Now we would like you to rate how important these services are to you, with 1 being not important and 100 being the most important. Then for each area of services, note why or why not these services are important to you.

How important is it to receive these services?	Importance 1 to 100

Investment Management
Why/Why Not?   _____

Estate Planning
Why/Why Not?   _____

Tax Planning and Preparation
Why/Why Not?   _____

Wealth Protection Services
(for all types of insurances)   _____
Why/Why Not?

Charitable Planning
Why/Why Not?   _____

with tax professionals in other parts of California. If you live outside of California and you are looking for a tax professional to help you, we encourage you to talk with your family, friends and co-workers to get a referral of someone they can recommend.

Some women told us they had concerns about their tax professional and were interested in switching to a new person. The biggest concerns our women clients tell us about their tax professionals are related to customer service. There are things such as not responding to voicemails and emails in a timely manner, and not completing work when they committed. Unless you have a relatively simple situation and are doing your taxes yourself, we feel it is very important that you have a relationship with a tax professional that you feel is doing a good job and is helping you reach your goals. You deserve it!

Insurance agents include professionals to help you with home, health, auto, life and long-term care insurances. We find this is sometimes an area that is overlooked. Some women may not have a specific person to help them with some areas of their insurances. Others may not have talked with their insurance agents for many years.

There are many different problems that can occur if a person has the wrong type of insurance, the wrong level of coverage or some type of insurance is missing altogether. We recommend having an insurance agent you can trust for each of these types of insurances. Since we are licensed life insurance agents and can help our clients with life insurance and long-term care insurance, we believe strongly in the value of having the appropriate insurances as part of your risk management for problems that can happen during your retirement.

Finally, charitable giving is an area that is sometimes a lower priority for some women when they are planning for retirement. There are some excellent strategies for making charitable giving easier, making sure money gets to the charities of your choice, while still providing the tax benefits that are legally allowed. We also find that women have varying levels of interest and priority for charitable giving.

What is important here is finding a strategy that makes it easy and tax efficient for you to contribute to the charities of your choice. There are so many excellent charities that need money and volunteer time for them to be successful. We encourage you to build a charitable giving plan that helps you reach your goals. If you are not sure on the best way to do this, we encourage you to work with a financial professional.

Whenever possible, we want to help our women clients build a team of outstanding professionals that they can count on and that will help them reach their goals. We like to work collaboratively to create a true team of experienced, high-quality professionals that are committed to helping our women clients reach their goals.

We have built systems to make it easier to work collaboratively with other professionals. This includes using a secure, electronic client vault, where we place investment statements (with the approval of our clients) so tax professionals can gather financial documents necessary to complete the tax returns. We also have the estate attorneys for our clients upload a copy of their estate documents to the vault, so they are in a safe and secure location that is easy for clients to access.

Your team may include a financial professional, estate attorney, insurance agents, a Professional Fiduciary, primary medical provider,

Professional Team

Instructions: In this exercise, we want you to identify the names of the professionals you currently have helping you in these important areas. Note whether you are happy with this person, or if you would prefer to work with someone you might like better. Where there is a role missing, or you are not happy with the person, note your actions for finding a professional in this area.

Financial Professional (name): _____

Am I happy with this person? _____

If not, why? Next steps? _____

Estate Attorney (name): _____

Am I happy with this person? _____

If not, why? Next steps? _____

Insurance Agent(s) (name): _____

Am I happy with this person? _____

If not, why? Next steps? _____

Fiduciary (name): _____

Am I happy with this person? _____

If not, why? Next steps? _____

Medicare Specialist (name): _____

Am I happy with this person? _____

If not, why? Next steps? _____

Other (name): _____

Am I happy with this person? _____

If not, why? Next steps? _____

create a Wealth Management firm that was designed from the beginning to serve our clients in the best ways possible. In 2018, we started Financial Journey Partners, located in San Jose, California. Elaine feels blessed and honored every day to work with so many amazing clients.

START PLANNING FOR RETIREMENT NOW

If you are still working, we encourage you to start planning NOW! You may be thinking of retiring this year. You may be planning to retire in the next 5 years. You may be younger and still have many years left before retiring. In any of these cases, we think you should start planning for retirement NOW! Even if you are many years away from retirement, we recommend that you have an investing plan in place to make sure you have enough money saved to complete the goals of your dreams during your retirement.

Our experience has shown us that there are unique needs and issues specific to women when you plan and implement your retirement. We hope that we have given you things to think about as we shared the words of wisdom and experiences from other successful women.

The exercises at the end of each chapter were designed to help you identify the things you can do to make your retirement even better. To make it easier to complete the exercises, we have created an electronic workbook for the exercises. You can download a complimentary workbook at our website www.financialjourney.com/books.

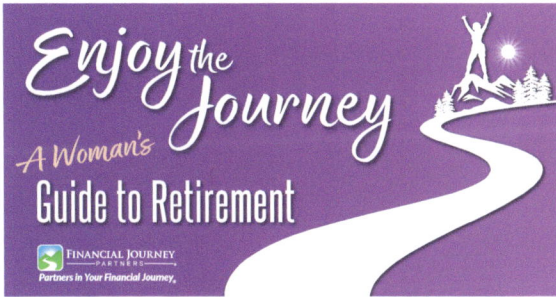

Enjoy the Journey
A Woman's Guide to Retirement

FINANCIAL JOURNEY
PARTNERS
Partners in Your Financial Journey.

W O R K B O O K

CLICK HERE TO GET STARTED

Elaine Manley, Founder & Wealth Manager, elaine@financialjourney.com
Scott Manley, Wealth Manager, scott@financialjourney.com
Linda Tjiuutra, Wealth Manager, linda@financialjourney.com

FinancialJourney.com | 408.963.2858

Partners in Your Financial Journey.
Investment advisory services offered through Mutual Advisors, LLC DBA Financial Journey Partners, a SEC registered investment adviser. Securities offered through Mutual Securities, Inc., member FINRA/SIPC. Mutual Securities, Inc. and Mutual Advisors, LLC are affiliated companies.

Another tool to help you plan your retirement is the FJP Retirement Framework™. This process is explained in more detail in our book ***Enjoy the Journey – Successful Retirement Strategies and Stories***. We created the FJP Retirement Framework™ as a roadmap to guide you on your journey. It is an excellent complement to this book and will give you more detailed information to help you with your retirement plan.

sensitive to how they are treated. They are appreciative of the extra time we spend identifying other professionals to round out their team. These are professionals that have more empathy and can explain things well, without "talking down" to someone.

We completely understand that this is about so much more than money for you and your family. We will challenge and support you to think about bigger possibilities that are aligned with who you are. Our goal is to help our clients make smart financial decisions and help them implement those decisions as smoothly as possible. Our team provides an exceptional level of service for our clients. At Financial Journey Partners, we work with a select group of families that are looking for a long-term relationship with a Wealth Manager. For our clients, we want to be *Partners in Your Financial Journey®*.

We host educational and fun events throughout the year to build a sense of community for our clients. It is an opportunity for clients to talk with other families that may be in similar situations. Since many clients refer their friends and family members, our client events provide opportunities for our other clients to get together with their family and friends, who are also clients. We even have an FJP Women's Group to encourage that sense of community among our women clients, and find enjoyable activities to do together like Pickleball, hiking in our beautiful area, and more.

We have been working with clients for decades. We are known for helping our clients make smart decisions so they can align their money with their goals and *Enjoy the Journey* along the way. Smart decisions are based on a deeper understanding of what and who is important to you.

It enables us to help guide you, whether through conversations or scenario planning, to help you make the best choices. What we mean by *Enjoy the Journey* is making sure you do the things you've been wanting to do, and possibly sooner rather than later. We want our clients to *Enjoy the Journey* along the way but think it through and make sure the timing is right for you.

If you're ready to start now to plan your financial future, you can schedule a complimentary introductory meeting with us on our website at www.financialjourney.com or call us at 408-963-2858. If we can help you, we'll let you know, and if we are not the right fit, we will do our best to introduce you to someone that might be a better fit to help you.

There are unique risks, challenges, goals and dreams for women. Let's celebrate what is unique for you and create a future that is exciting and full of possibility. We want you to live the life of your dreams. We want you to achieve your goals and accomplish more than you ever considered possible. Think big! Dream big! Then create a plan to achieve it all. And remember, along the way, we encourage you to *Enjoy the Journey!*

To your future!
Elaine and Scott Manley

Appendix 1

https://www.forbes.com/advisor/retirement/sequence-of-returns-risk/

www.financialjourney.com/books

https://www.dmv.ca.gov/portal/news-and-media/dmv-now-offers-online-drivers-license-testing-options/

Volunteermatch.org

Cogenerate.org

NPS.gov/getinvolved/volunteer.htm

Appendix 2

In late 2023, we surveyed our women clients who are 55 and older, to get their views and experiences related to their retirement. Sixty women responded to the survey. The analysis of the survey results is spread through throughout the chapters of this book. This is a summary of the answers to each question.

1. Whether you are planning for retirement and you are still working, or you have already retired, what is your biggest concern when you think about your retirement?

    41% - Staying healthy to live a long and active life

    24% - Running out of money

    20% - Not being a financial burden on my family or friends when I get older

    17% - Maintaining the lifestyle that I had while working after I retire

    8% - Other

2. What do you think is the number one thing that you are most concerned about from living the retirement of your dreams?

    46% - Health issues including dementia

    24% - Running out of money

    30% - Other (Living too long, inflation, taxes, political issues, major stock market crash

Special Thanks

We are grateful for all the people that have helped us with the creation of this book. Special thanks to Scott's sister, Paula Manley, who helped us with multiple rounds of editing this book and with providing many helpful suggestions. We also want to thank Karen Duncum for her guidance and knowledge. Her section on goal setting in Chapter 6 helps you expand what you thought was possible. We encourage you to get these goals into your calendar.

Other people we would like to thank are John Bowen and Jon Powell and the team at CEG. This group is dedicated to helping Wealth Managers create a fantastic experience for their clients. They also help us improve our business processes. We are grateful for all their help and support over the years.

Thank you, Nick Fryer, for the beautiful graphics on the cover and inside the book. Thank you, Mario Fachini, for guiding us on the development and distribution of our book.

We really appreciate our women clients who have allowed us to tell their inspiring and uplifting stories of how they have worked hard, planned well, and won the game of life. We also want to thank the amazing team at Financial Journey Partners that works very hard every day to give our clients a great experience.

About the Authors

Elaine Manley

Elaine is the founder and the senior Wealth Manager at Financial Journey Partners. She paid for her college education by working in a co-op program at General Motors Institute, where she got her bachelor's degree in finance and industrial administration. She started her career in the Accounting Department at a General Motors division in the Midwest. One day with the wind chill hitting 35 below zero, Elaine decided to move to warmer weather. Having been to Silicon Valley a year earlier and loving the area, she chose to move to Sunnyvale, CA and began working in the Accounting Department at Hewlett-Packard.

Elaine decided quickly that her passion was not to work for a large corporation. She found it much more important to help improve people's lives and help them achieve their goals and dreams. She started her career as a financial advisor at a national financial firm. Over the years, she became one of the most respected and successful financial advisors at the firm.

When Elaine and Scott started their new firm in 2018, they wanted to create a firm that was different from other financial firms, building on their decades of experience. They wanted their clients to see them as *Partners in Your Financial Journey®*. Scott designed the new office for Financial Journey Partners to create the ideal space that is comfortable and inviting for clients to plan and implement their goals and dreams. Financial Journey Partners has an amazing and experienced team to provide a high level of service to our clients.

Elaine and Scott are excited every day to come to work and help their clients reach their goals and *Enjoy the Journey* along the way. Elaine and Scott feel blessed to have in their lives so many wonderful people that are clients and friends, and for them, this is how they *Enjoy the Journey*.

This book is designed to be practical and inspirational and help you make smart decisions as you *Enjoy the Journey*. Start your journey today!

Milton Keynes UK
Ingram Content Group UK Ltd.
UKHW052234011124
450426UK00001B/1